MY JOURNEY Journal

Capturing Stories Through Time

A personal collection of thoughts, insights, and cultural narratives

Willka's publications may be purchased for educational, business, or sales promotion use.

For more information, please write:
Willka Publishing LLC
5421 Highway 100, Unit 58952
Nashville, TN 37205

ISBN: 979-8-9912253-4-2

Distributed by Willka Publishing LLC
5421 Highway 100, Unit 58952
Nashville, TN 37205

First Edition, 2025.

Welcome to your personal journey. This journal is designed to work alongside you as you navigate and achieve imagine and achieve your goals.

This journal is your sacred space to capture your vision, break down ambitious goals into actionable steps, celebrate your wins, and chart your path forward. It is designed to work alongside you as you navigate and achieve your goals, building a foundation of lifelong habits, and positive joy as you work through each prompt.

The Power of Consistency is dedicated time each day (as little as 5-10 minutes) to YOU! Focusing on yourself isn't selfish—it's essential to building life-changing habits and maintaining intentional focus on your goals. You thrive when you prioritize your wellbeing.

I encourage you to reflect on your journaling each week. Setting aside time to review your goals will empower you to move confidently toward the life you envision. Remember—you're not just building a career and family, you're crafting a legacy.

Your journey matters. Your voice matters. Your vision matters.

I look forward to being on this journey with you.

Warmly,

Michele

Gratitude and attitude are not *challenges*.

They are **choices**.

Robert Braathe

Today

Date

GOAL:

TOP 3 TASKS

1.
2.
3.

AFFIRMATIONS FOR THIS WEEK

TO DO'S ON MY MIND

Gratitude

Date

Today I am grateful for....

Date

Date

Simply *start* with knowing what you don't want to move *forward*.

Today

Date

GOAL:

TOP 3 TASKS

1.
2.
3.

AFFIRMATIONS FOR THIS WEEK

TO DO'S ON MY MIND

Gratitude

Date

Today I am grateful for....

Date

Date

NEVER FORGET HOW

wildly

CAPABLE YOU ARE.

Today

Date

GOAL:

TOP 3 TASKS

1.
2.
3.

AFFIRMATIONS FOR THIS WEEK

TO DO'S ON MY MIND

Gratitude

Date

Today I am grateful for....

Date

Date

Start each day

with a grateful heart

Today

Date

GOAL:

TOP 3 TASKS

1.
2.
3.

AFFIRMATIONS FOR THIS WEEK

TO DO'S ON MY MIND

Gratitude

Date

Today I am grateful for....

Date

Gratitude

Date

Today I am grateful for....

Date

Date

Cultivate an attitude of gratefulness

Write about one person you are grateful to have influenced your life.

When I started counting my blessings, my whole life turned around.
~ Willie Nelson ~

There are so many beautiful reasons to be *happy*.

Today

Date

GOAL:

TOP 3 TASKS

1.
2.
3.

AFFIRMATIONS FOR THIS WEEK

TO DO'S ON MY MIND

Gratitude

Date

Today I am grateful for....

Date

Date

Be Bold

Say what you want **before** it is too late.

Be bold and let your *truest* friends find **YOU**.

Today

Date

GOAL:

TOP 3 TASKS

1.
2.
3.

AFFIRMATIONS FOR THIS WEEK

TO DO'S ON MY MIND

Gratitude

Date

Today I am grateful for....

Date

Date

where you are *right* now.

Date

GOAL:

TOP 3 TASKS

1.
2.
3.

AFFIRMATIONS FOR THIS WEEK

TO DO'S ON MY MIND

Gratitude

Date

Today I am grateful for....

Date

Date

The **best** time for
new beginnings is

NOW

Today

Date

GOAL:

TOP 3 TASKS

1.
2.
3.

AFFIRMATIONS FOR THIS WEEK

TO DO'S ON MY MIND

Gratitude

Date

Today I am grateful for....

Date

Date

Gratitude

Date

Cultivate an attitude of gratefulness

Write about finding beauty or joy in things that are imperfect. Why do you find them more interesting or impactful?

When we focus on our gratitude, the tide of disappointment goes out and the tide of love rushes in.
~ Kristin Armstrong ~

What's coming

is *better*

than what's **gone**

Today

Date

GOAL:

TOP 3 TASKS

1.
2.
3.

AFFIRMATIONS FOR THIS WEEK

TO DO'S ON MY MIND

Gratitude

Date

Today I am grateful for....

Date

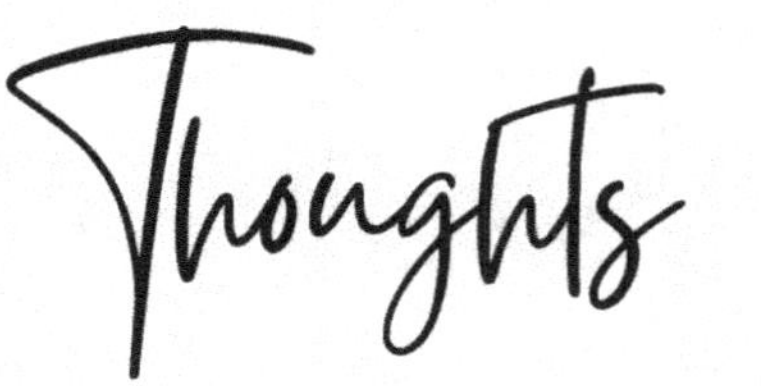

Date

Be **OBSESSED**

with your ***own*** potential.

Today

Date

GOAL:

TOP 3 TASKS

1.
2.
3.

AFFIRMATIONS FOR THIS WEEK

TO DO'S ON MY MIND

Gratitude

Date

Today I am grateful for....

Date

Date

Strive for forward progress,
not perfection.

Today

Date

GOAL:

TOP 3 TASKS

1.
2.
3.

AFFIRMATIONS FOR THIS WEEK

TO DO'S ON MY MIND

Gratitude

Date

Today I am grateful for....

Date

Date

Celebrate the **WINS**

no matter how *small*

Today

Date

GOAL:

TOP 3 TASKS

1.
2.
3.

AFFIRMATIONS FOR THIS WEEK

TO DO'S ON MY MIND

Gratitude

Date

Today I am grateful for....

Date

Date

Date

Cultivate an attitude of gratefulness.

Write one highlight of gratefulness this week.

Joyous moments are worth collecting!

SOME PEOPLE ARE THERE FOR A SEASON,

but always a reason.

Today

Date

GOAL:

TOP 3 TASKS

1.
2.
3.

AFFIRMATIONS FOR THIS WEEK

TO DO'S ON MY MIND

Gratitude

Date

Today I am grateful for....

Date

Date

I can't think of any better representation of beauty than someone who is *unafraid* to be **herself**.

Emma Stone

Today

Date

GOAL:

TOP 3 TASKS

1.
2.
3.

AFFIRMATIONS FOR THIS WEEK

TO DO'S ON MY MIND

Gratitude

Date

Today I am grateful for....

Date

Date

Never be **afraid** to fall apart because it's an opportunity to rebuild yourself the way you wish you had been all along.

Rae Smith

Today

Date

GOAL:

TOP 3 TASKS

1.
2.
3.

AFFIRMATIONS FOR THIS WEEK

TO DO'S ON MY MIND

Gratitude

Date

Today I am grateful for....

Thoughts
Date

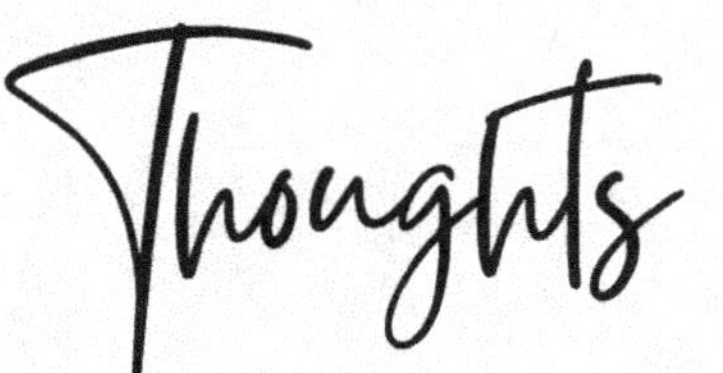

Date

Don't let your calendar control **YOU**.

You decide how productive your days are. Some people need a packed schedule to feel accomplished. Others achieve a year's worth of results in just one week of focused work.

Today

Date

GOAL:

TOP 3 TASKS

1.
2.
3.

AFFIRMATIONS FOR THIS WEEK

TO DO'S ON MY MIND

Gratitude

Date

Today I am grateful for....

Date

Date

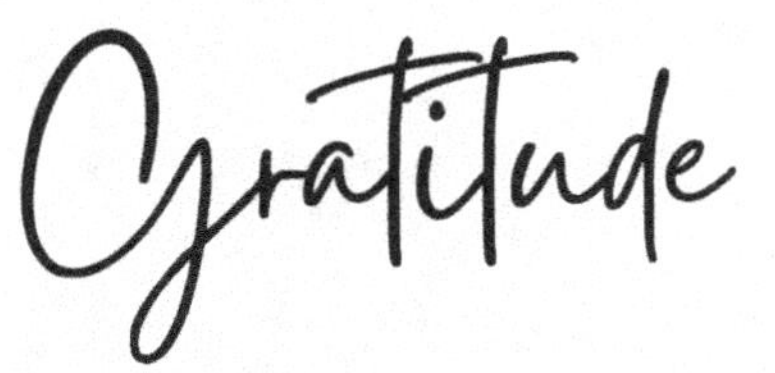

Date

Cultivate an attitude of gratefulness

Write about an experience that you are grateful for that shaped who you are today.

The most important thing is to enjoy your life...
to be happy...it's all that matters.
~ Audrey Hepburn ~

Action is the *foundational* key to **all** success.

Picasso

Today

Date

GOAL:

TOP 3 TASKS

1.
2.
3.

AFFIRMATIONS FOR THIS WEEK

TO DO'S ON MY MIND

Gratitude

Date

Today I am grateful for....

Date

Thoughts

Date

Meryl Streep

Date

GOAL:

TOP 3 TASKS

1.
2.
3.

AFFIRMATIONS FOR THIS WEEK

TO DO'S ON MY MIND

Date

Date

Don't count the days,
make the days COUNT!

Muhammed Ali

Today

Date

GOAL:

TOP 3 TASKS

1.
2.
3.

AFFIRMATIONS FOR THIS WEEK

TO DO'S ON MY MIND

Gratitude

Date

Today I am grateful for....

Date

Date

The world belongs to the

ENTHUSIASTIC.

Ralph Waldo Emerson

Today

Date

GOAL:

TOP 3 TASKS

1.
2.
3.

AFFIRMATIONS FOR THIS WEEK

TO DO'S ON MY MIND

Gratitude

Date

Today I am grateful for....

Date

Date

Date

Cultivate an attitude of gratefulness

Sometimes the smallest things take up
the most room in your heart.
~ Winnie the Pooh ~

What small things are on your heart?
Are they holding you back or moving you forward?

Acknowledging the good that you already have in
your life is the foundation for all abundance.
~ Eckhart Tolle ~

IT ALWAYS SEEMS IMPOSSIBLE

until it's done.

Nelson Mandela

Date

GOAL:

TOP 3 TASKS

1.
2.
3.

AFFIRMATIONS FOR THIS WEEK

TO DO'S ON MY MIND

Gratitude

Date

Today I am grateful for....

Date

Date

The secret of getting ahead is getting started.

Mark Twain

Today

Date

GOAL:

TOP 3 TASKS

1.
2.
3.

AFFIRMATIONS FOR THIS WEEK

TO DO'S ON MY MIND

Gratitude

Date

Today I am grateful for....

Date

Date

Build your own dreams,
or someone else will hire
you to build theirs.

Farrah Gray

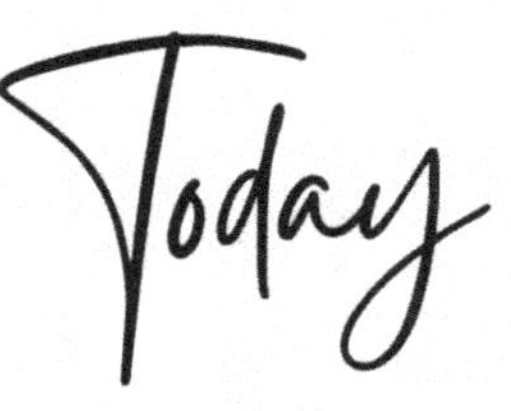

Date

GOAL:

TOP 3 TASKS

1.
2.
3.

AFFIRMATIONS FOR THIS WEEK

TO DO'S ON MY MIND

Gratitude

Date

Today I am grateful for....

Date

Date

The question is...

Who is going to STOP me?

Today

Date

GOAL:

TOP 3 TASKS

1.
2.
3.

AFFIRMATIONS FOR THIS WEEK

TO DO'S ON MY MIND

Gratitude

Date

Today I am grateful for....

Date

Date

We are so grateful you've chosen this journal to support your journey of growth and self-discovery. Every word you write is a step forward, and we are honored to be part of your path.

Your commitment to yourself is inspiring—never forget how powerful small, consistent steps can be. Keep going - You are worth it!

Michele + The Willka Team

To receive a free downloadable tool each month, find additional resources, or to book Michele at your next speaking event, please visit our website at www.micheleoglesby.com or email us directly at hello@willka.co

willka
journey

$15.99
ISBN 979-8-9912253-4-2

www.ingramcontent.com/pod-product-compliance
Lightning Source LLC
Chambersburg PA
CBHW080903120626
46555CB00008B/2926
* 9 7 9 8 9 9 1 2 2 5 3 4 2 *